Contents

1   Today's Situation 2

2   Working Capital Reporting 5

3   Collections 8

4   Dispute Management 11

5   The Remaining Receivables 14

6   Inventory Management 17

7   The Remaining Inventories 21

8   Supplier Payment Terms 24

9   Payment Timing 27

10   Supply Chain Finance 30

11   Vision 33

About the Author 36

Contacts 37

Preface

It has been a long held belief in business that having no working capital is only realistic in certain exceptional circumstances. The first is that you have very low working capital because you are a retailer that is paid immediately, manages stocks well and pays suppliers very slowly. Whilst this can certainly be true, it is also true that outside of retailers the vast majority of companies are resigned to the fact that working capital exists and that it must be funded. And yet there are non-retailers who have eliminated working capital and even report consistent negative working capital. So I wondered about what was stopping other companies from achieving the same thing. Even if you still believe zero working capital to be impossible then I would argue that achieving half of that target is still a worthwhile achievement.

In this booklet I look at each element of working capital and the actions that can be taken in pursuit of zero working capital. For some companies some of these steps will be unnecessary since they already do these things or they will never have any need. Other solutions will prove to be unavailable to others. There will be a final group of companies who could do all of these things from a technical perspective but they are not yet ready for such change.

As with my other publications, I will do my best to avoid jargon and if I have failed in that endeavour I humbly apologise in advance. In the meantime I hope that this small volume will help you to improve working capital management at your company.

1 Today's Situation

The principles of working capital management have not changed but the tools that allow us to do that job efficiently have changed dramatically over the last 40 years. Back in the 1970's we did not have personal computers, it was difficult to do any kind of intelligent analysis. Back then working capital management meant attacking accounts receivable with a calling campaign supported by manually written index cards to record activity and diarise follow-ups. The most advanced reports available might be an aged debt report. Payables was only one step above cheque cutting. Many systems did not store payment terms so they could not be managed on a systematic basis in a large environment. The principles of statistical inventory management had been long established, but systems were not available that could give the real time information that supply chain managers required to intelligently manage their portfolios. And then came the technology revolution that has impacted the entire finance and manufacturing world. The introduction of ERP systems gave the promise that large amounts of data could be stored, extracted and turned into information for decision makers. The personal computer, with associated spreadsheet and database tools, was supposed to be the vehicle by which we could do most of this analysis. But we found that it was very difficult to extract data from these ERP systems. The spreadsheets and databases created a plethora of non-standard reporting that was difficult to maintain or replicate and even more difficult to compare from one report author to the next. The ERP vendors very kindly bolted on report writing tools to their ERP systems to help resolve the problem. But companies found it difficult to find people with both the technical skills to build reports and the business acumen to design these reports. Over the years the ERP vendors have developed even more advanced solutions to the same problem without significant resolution. Businesses have continued on in the imperfect world of spreadsheets and databases, now supplemented by non-ERP software vendors who have produced a range of both good and bad middleware tools that have increased most businesses capability to report on working capital issues and then create sustainable specialist processes to deal with specific problems.

When we look at the working capital results that these companies have produced over the last 20 years we find that while many have improved, an equal number have declined. The real story for many companies is that working capital results have been inconsistent. Business events happen that mean a perfectly well managed working capital portfolio has been blown off course. One of the biggest reasons for this has been merger and acquisition activity. You would think that companies that are better at managing working capital will be in a better position to be the acquirer but very often this has not been true. The truth is that those companies that have intelligently managed debt have been the big winners. Money has been borrowed at relatively cheap rates to acquire vast amounts of assets. And the bigger the company the more likely it is that banks want to offer debt. So many big companies are awash with liquidity and many smaller companies have been starved of liquidity. But even for those larger companies things are changing. The vast majority of banks have been shown to have been reckless in their dealings for many years and even seven years after the collapse of Lehmann Brothers banks are still repairing their balance sheets. This has meant that if you are a mega large company with an excellent debt rating, and there are not that many left, the banks are falling over themselves to lend you money. This also means that many companies who were lent large sums in the past are under increasing pressure to pay back debt or roll-over their debts to another bank. For some of these companies this has been the trigger to finally address their own working capital issues. Managing working capital well means that you have access to the cheapest form of funding on the market. For smaller companies it is even harder to get working capital funding. This itself creates new opportunities as more solutions come to the marketplace.

In conjunction with that fact there are now many excellent tools and techniques available to almost all companies, ignorance is no longer a defence for poor working capital management. All the reports from the Big 4 and others tell us that the working capital average for most large companies is in a range of 10% to 16%. If they are right then there is the potential to shrink this percentage range by about half. For many that would be an amazing thing to achieve, but the gap between the very best and the mid range is widening all the time. So in the following sections I will focus on those that are the very best and those about to become the very best. What are the things they are doing, beyond being lucky, that mean that they can be the best at working capital management. The first thing is the target. The target of the very best is zero. That's right. No working capital at all. It seems unbelievable but the fact remains that there are a handful of companies that have achieved this on a consistent basis and there are more who share this as an ambition.

2 Working Capital Reporting

You can't manage what you don't measure. That is a statement that has long been true and when applied to the issue of working capital management has meant that only a small minority of companies really know what is going on. You would rightly ask how this can be the case after the same companies spent billions over the years implementing ERP systems. The truth is that these ERP systems have been excellent in allowing businesses to grow into multi-million and even multi-billion transactional players but have done almost nothing to help companies build decent reporting suites that would have solved the reporting problem. It is also true that many of these ERP products require external IT consultants, very often big 4 firms, to configure these systems to your company's specific needs. It turns out that most of the reporting products that they produce also need another bunch of consultants to come in to design and configure these reports. This is now called a Business Intelligence project.

The remarkable thing is that some companies have done this multiple times. For example, many years ago SAP had a reporting product called Business Warehouse. It worked very well as long as you had someone to configure the reports that also had a decent knowledge of the business requirement. Unfortunately, if you had someone with the IT skills to build the reports but did not have the business experience of someone who understood the business requirement, you ended up with pretty but often useless reports. In the opposite case where you had someone with the right business experience but without the necessary IT skills you ended up with no reports at all. Then SAP bought Business Objects. They claimed that it was superior to Business Warehouse and made it core to their product set. So now all those people who had developed reports in Business Warehouse had to rewrite them in Business Objects. And there was still the problem of IT skills and business experience described earlier. Now SAP has decided to embrace "Big Data" and have developed a product called HANA. HANA is far superior technologically than anything that came before it, but again the day that you get HANA there are no reports. They must be built in a similar fashion to what happened with the older products. This has now become a key growth area for Big 4 consultants where they come to you to design and implement this new super intelligent reporting suite - at a price. These business intelligence projects are very expensive and very often fall short of the quality mark since most IT consultants have a limited understanding of real business needs. To be fair to SAP, all the other major ERP platform providers have pursued a similar strategy that has delivered identical results.

Because of all this the finance community has resorted to its trusted friend - the spreadsheet. When I started in finance, spreadsheets where a nice way of displaying tabular information. I remember being told many times that spreadsheets were fine as a short term solution but could never be considered to be a robust transferable solution. But instead of limiting the application of the spreadsheet, the spreadsheet has been transformed. First we learned how to extract large amounts of data from our accounting systems. Then we put them in enormous spreadsheets and databases, wrote macros to try and make sense of the data, created lookup tables to analyse the results and made the whole thing completely unintelligible and very difficult to repeat. This is an affliction of many finance departments and has a strong impact on working capital management. This is either because the reporting takes so much time to produce that it limits the amount of time and effort that is available for finance departments to do anything about the working capital result or the reports are not taken seriously by the business.

For example, at a Shared Service Centre in Poland a huge percentage of daily activity is spent on extracting data to make pretty reports for the business. These reports are then posted to the company's intranet so they are available for all the relevant people to read. But there is no evidence that anyone reads the reports. So this could be a lot of effort wasted. If you find yourself in this situation, I would recommend that for the first month you continue to produce all usual reports but only send those reports to people on request. In the second month stop producing the unrequested reports altogether. You would be amazed how much time is then freed up to do far more productive things.

There are many products out there that have shown that it does not have to be the way of SAP and Big 4 consultants and that these things are within the grasp of much smaller companies. A favourite of mine is a product called CashForce by DiscoverEdge in Belgium. These guys have put together the single best working capital reporting suite that I have yet seen. There is a plethora of standard reports that feed directly from the data tables in your ERP system, you can do all sorts of ad-hoc reporting, it can be used as a data extraction tool, it simulates results based on targets that you input, forecasts cash flows and can even be used as a credit collection tool. The real difference is that this software is equally attainable by small and large businesses that can then avail of best practice reporting without big license fees for software or big consulting bills. This is a revolution within your grasp right now!

3 Collections

Best practice collections has always been about focusing on the right customers and then doing the right thing with those customers. So the start point is to segment your customer base. Traditionally most businesses will focus on calling the largest customers first and that is quite right. But best practice would also say that you should behave differently depending on the payment behaviour of the customer.

Segmentation done this way will mean that you end up with a 9-box segmentation where one axis is based on the size of the customer's revenue (A-B-C) where the A's are the largest customers. The other axis is based on payment behaviour (1-2-3) where the 1's are those who pay you either early or up to due date, the 2's are those customers that pay just after due date and the 3's are those that pay you long after due date. From a collection perspective you might think the 3's are the hardest to deal with, but that is not true.

Most people would think that the 3's are businesses that are trying to dodge their bills and are just giving excuses not to pay. There is no doubt that there are a number who are exactly like this but they tend to be a small minority. More of the 3's are businesses who have very poor internal processes which could be around the approval of invoices or their payment process. Either way these are the customers that you need to be in constant contact with every month, possibly on several occasions, to ensure that you are getting promises to pay and that they are being fulfilled. I call these customers the "little children" of collections activity. For those of you who have or have had small children you will have vast experience of giving the same instruction multiple times before the instruction is executed. The good news is that children grow up and get to a point where multiple communication of instructions is no longer required. However a business with very poor internal processes will never grow up without significant change on their end. In the meantime it is incumbent on the collector to call this type of customer continuously to ensure that promised actions actually happen. It is annoying to have to do this but it is not difficult.

On the other hand the 2's are masters of process. These are the customers who pay consistently up to 4 to 5 days after due date. They know exactly what they are doing. Very often these are the businesses that transmit payment on the due date and make sure that you do not receive the cash in your bank until several days afterwards. In the US these are the customers who will pay by cheque on third class post to a drop-box in Alaska. With these customers the risk of default is almost nil but it is almost certain that you will be paid after due date. You can change their ways through negotiation, but a collector will need the help of sales to change any of these hard-coded behaviours. Collectors have to work hard on these accounts to learn the customer's internal process and make sure that no-one trips a switch somewhere in the total process that will result in an invoice being paid late.

There are a few businesses that have a handful of customers that can all be reached on a personal basis. In large businesses this is extremely rare so the collection call focus should be on a maximum of four sectors of our 9-box grid: A2 (large slightly late) , A3 (large very late) , B2 (medium slightly late) and B3 (medium very late). The idea is that the collectors are then allocated accounts to call from these groups. This should also ensure that we have 90-95% ledger coverage by value from our collector team. That will mean that our collectors are capable of making a difference to the result.

Collectors must also have the right tools. Increasingly this means collection software that understands the segmentation, allocates the accounts to collectors, records promises or issues raised by customers and diarises calls and follow-ups. There are many good tools out there some of which are very expensive and complicated and others that are cheap and simplistic but the all broadly do the same thing. These tools keep collectors disciplined and allow managers to monitor activity on a daily basis. This allows managers to take any necessary corrective action more proactively and not after month end results come up short.

There must also be a more automated way of reaching smaller customers. This is called dunning. This involves sending automated letters or emails to customers to remind them that payment is late and that action will be taken if no payment is received. There are many in business who believe that dunning is a waste of time since so many people ignore them. I do not agree with this viewpoint but these folks do have a valid point in that poorly designed letters or emails or empty threats to customers will not be effective in collecting cash. The first step is that letters need to stand out and be noticed. Many do not and as a result go in the "round filing cabinet" immediately. Secondly, if you say you are going to stop supply or some other threat if payment is not made then you need to carry through with that threat. If not, your collection process will be undermined and the customer will learn that you are not really serious. This is why sales and customer service need to be fully bought in to the process so that process discipline is fully maintained.

4 Dispute Management

Although the subject of dispute management has moved on leaps and bounds in the last 20 years, it is still far too common that I hold my head in my hands when I see companies that have spent a small fortune on ERP systems and yet have no means of dealing with customer disputes or deductions in an efficient manner. What they also miss is the ability to quantify the errors that occur in the business and the chance to improve the business by eliminating those errors from their business process. So to be in line with best practice dispute management and have that capability of improving your business there are seven clear steps that you need to follow.

The first step is to clearly identify that a dispute or a deduction has happened. It is unfortunately very common that disputes are not detected until it is too late to prevent late payment. This will always be true in cases where the customer contact is after the due date but is also common with customers who have many deductions that are only detected when their cash remittance is received. In each of these cases the potential that the dispute could have been resolved before due date has been missed. It is very common that when professional collectors start calling customers for the first time that the level of disputes goes up. This is not because collection calls cause disputes, but because these disputes were buried somewhere in the process. So surfacing of disputes goes very much hand in hand with proactive collection calling.

The next step is to categorise the type of dispute. There are usually a relatively small group of issues that cause disputes. Examples would be billing errors due to wrong pricing, quantities and tax calculations. There could be delivery related problems such as damaged goods, wrong delivery location, product substitution or missed delivery time-slot. In service related industries there could be issues about timesheets, installation sign-offs, recharged expenses and so on. There should never be a list of more than 20 categories. If there are more than this then reporting will become too granular and the big picture might be missed. Equally, if there are too few categories then the reporting will not be granular enough and then reporting will not be meaningful.

It is important to assign the dispute to a specific person in the business and not to a group or department. This is important since we must be able to ascertain who is accountable for the resolution of a dispute. If we do not identify and individual then there is the possibility of people passing the buck to others. If escalated this can then become a "he says, she says" argument that will be difficult to resolve internally.

Disputes need to be tracked in order that they come to a successful resolution in a reasonable timescale. So the first thing we will need is a means of tracking who has been assigned which disputes. Each dispute type should be given a standard time to resolution that reflects the difficulty in agreeing the action that will resolve that dispute. For example, pricing errors are usually an administrative problem either with your customer service department or with your customers ordering department and can usually be sorted in a few days. On the other hand a serious contractual dispute that may have lawyers involved is likely to take significantly longer.

Resolution of a dispute needs to be resolved with a corresponding action. For example, if you had a price dispute with the customer and the resolution was that their company needed to update their pricing file to the correct prices, then you would also expect a promise to pay for the amount that was disputed. If that promise to pay was not given then it is likely that the supposed resolution was not communicated to the customer. If this is the case, then the disputed amount will continue not to be paid.

The ultimate goal of a dispute management process is to eliminate these errors from the business process. This will require working with customers and internal stakeholders so that joint solutions can be found. Very often this might happen on a customer by customer basis, but when a solution is found then there is an opportunity to offer that solution to other customers.

There are cases where the dispute issue will repeat itself. For example in the meat industry there is a specific dispute type called drippage. This happens because fresh meat is always decreasing in weight due to the water content dripping out of the meat. So when the meat is shipped it is weighed and thus an invoice is produced for that weight. When delivered the customer will weigh the product and will always be lighter. At one client they correctly identified the problem but then had to manually deal with each dispute raised. In every case the dispute was accepted and credited. In cases like this the dispute approval should be automated. When dealing with large supermarkets the volume of such disputes can be gigantic. Automating the approval of such disputes can save a huge amount of work right across the business.

5 The Remaining Receivables

I was recently at a pharmaceutical company and I was asked why they should be offering extended terms to a Middle Eastern distributor when these were life changing drugs that were in very high demand. I'm not going to try and answer this point directly but it did get me thinking. I work with many companies that are trying to reduce payment terms with their customers and the biggest barrier they have are themselves. By that I mean that most organisations rarely ask this important question and if they do they quickly place the question in the "too difficult" category and move on to other things. But reducing customer terms can be done successfully if it is driven by sales and they get the right targeting information from finance.

Very often salespeople have very little idea of the payment terms that have been agreed with customers and even less idea of how customers pay to those terms. Recently at a client who sells to construction industry customers in the UK, we noticed that many smaller customers had been placed on 60 days terms even though company policy was to have a maximum of 30 days. The finance people were convinced that changing these customers back to 30 days would result in lost business and a huge amount of noise from sales. It turned out that they were completely wrong. We agreed that we would change these customers payment terms back to 30 days without telling sales or any formal communication to the customer. Out of approximately 500 customers affected, we got no response from sales or from the customers concerned. This goes to show not only that the sales people didn't really know the true payment terms for these accounts but that in many cases the customers didn't know either. This is not to make little of what can be a difficult subject but it does show that a lot can be done that feels very counter-intuitive without rocking the boat.

For smaller businesses or those with average credit ratings there is one final way of trying to wipe out your receivables balance and the answer is factoring, i.e. selling your receivables asset to a third party. This can take most of the remaining receivables balance off the books. It is usually banks that offer such products and they can be picky about what they buy. So they will try to exclude all receivables aged over a certain level, e.g. 90 days, or will exclude the balances from accounts that they consider too risky. Factoring is a very old concept and historically has been very successful in allowing smaller businesses to convert their receivables asset into cash flow very quickly. But remember that factoring comes at a price. For small businesses the usual business case is the balance between the interest costs that the bank will charge versus the cost of setting up a collection department of your own. In some cases where the answer to this balance is negative the small business might still elect to factor receivables since they need the liquidity in order to run their business. While this kind of factoring is commonly available in many countries it is usually an expensive way to gain liquidity.

A relatively new form of factoring is by using receivables exchanges. In this case you have the ability to sell individual invoices or blocks of invoices in a marketplace designed and run by the service provider. Potential buyers of your debt have the opportunity to bid for your invoices. Each bidder will set an interest rate that they will accept and the length of time of the deal. So a bidder might offer to buy your invoices for 20 days at an annualised interest rate of 5%. The marketplace software will then offer you a range of deals based on the rates being offered by the buyers and you choose a deal that is acceptable to your company. This kind of marketplace can work very well for small businesses that need the liquidity but want to get a rate that is cheaper than an overdraft from a bank. There are a number of these exchanges the largest of which is the US based Receivables Exchange. There have been numerous attempts to imitate the model in Europe that so far have not been successful. The problem for these companies is often that they are trying to convince small companies to go beyond their normal banking relationships. This is especially true in Europe where the rate of small businesses changing banks is very low.

One of the things that has become very evident since 2009 is that banks are looking for safer and safer ways to lend money in order to shore up the risk ratings of their own balance sheets. In two recent examples banks have approached global pharmaceutical companies to see if they want to sell their receivables at very low rates. I have seen this in both the USA and Japan where the probability of being paid is very high, the company in question has an excellent debt rating, and like most pharmaceutical companies, was producing phenomenal amounts of cash and really didn't need the assistance. Effectively the bank buys the receivables once they have been invoiced and then sells them back to the client a number of days before the due date. These deals are worth billions of dollars in cash and are very attractive to a high earning pharmaceutical company. So while such deals are available, they are only an option for those very large corporates with excellent cash flows and debt ratings who see this as an opportunity to get cash at a very cheap price to reinvest in their high margin businesses. But it does show that the gap between the opportunities open to the very top players and small businesses is continuing to grow.

6 Inventory Management

No matter who comes up with the latest new fangled idea the basics of inventory management do not change. Accountants will argue that they want inventory kept to a minimum and supply chain managers will never want to run out of stock. The reality is that inventory needs to be optimised. Having too much stock is a poor use of an asset, slows down business investment and increases the possibility of product obsolescence. Having too little stock will result in lost sales and possibly push the customer into the arms of a competitor. The reality is that there are a number more factors that are important to the final answer.

The first issue is the size of the product range. This can be a difficult thing to get right. In the fashion trade a key element is colour. So you might have the right garment but not all the colours will sell. In this trade, it means retailers will discount these items in their sales or scrap the remaining stock. So the narrower your range, assuming you have picked the right designs, the more profit the fashion retailer will make. The danger is that narrowing your range to items that no-one wants will cause sales to plunge. But there is a way of dealing with the problem. While working at a producer of laminate board, they told us that they always produced fourteen designs and that each of these designs would be available for a full year before bringing out the next fourteen designs. It was clear from their inventory data that stocks were amassing based on the designs in previous years that hadn't sold. We instituted a process where they would review sales of the entire range after three months and then make a decision to scale down or stop production of the less popular items. In a retail environment, a good retailer is always watching what the customer is buying often on a daily basis. Based on this information they then decide to reorder or not or to move out stock that is not selling and so on. Retailers can make these decisions very quickly. In a manufacturing environment the principle is the same but there must be a data stream in place so that a proper evaluation can be made.

Once the data is in place then it will be possible to quickly identify the big sellers from the lesser sellers, but it will also be possible to measure sales volatility. If your customers are ordering similar amounts at a similar frequency then this is said to be low volatility. Here there is an opportunity to reduce safety stocks and deliver a very high level of customer service. The customer service level is determined by the number of times you expect to fail the customer's expectation of delivery. You can never reach 100% service level as the statistics would determine that you would need an infinite amount of stock. So the idea is to set the service level at a point where it is appropriate for that product's demand profile. Another problem arises when you have a high volatility product that also has a high level of demand. If you make such items to stock and apply the same customer service level as the low volatility items you will end up with a huge amount of stock for these items. So the trick is to reduce the customer service level to something more reasonable. This will lower the amount of stock required to service the demand. In cases where the volatility level is extremely high then you might want to make the choice of not making to stock but instead making to order. This will inevitably drive up the lead time to the customer but is an effective way of balancing the inventory profile. As sales of a product drop toward the end of the product lifecycle it is common that demand becomes more erratic. So when you see this information in your data it can be an early sign that the product is about to become more slow moving. You can then take steps to decrease production, increase customer lead times or change your stocking policy to make to order. All these steps will reduce the level of obsolete stock that you might be left with over time.

But there is still a forecast of future demand to create. There are lots of forecasting techniques that can be used and it is important to use an appropriate method. For example, when at a frozen vegetable producer we found that the forecast was done once per year and then divided equally into weekly buckets over the course of the year. This was clearly wrong since it took no account either of the seasonality of sales or harvesting. The next problem with forecasting is the multiple forecast. That happens when different people in the organisation do not trust each other's inputs. It ends up with a supply chain planner "taking a view" on all these inputs based on whether he or she believes the inputs to be too optimistic or pessimistic. This is where you will often hear the term Sales and Operations Planning or "S&OP". S&OP is simply a transparent process where all inputs are provided openly and there is an agreed method that gets everyone to an agreed and transparent forecast. One advantage of such a process is that if an individual input is seen to be too optimistic or pessimistic, there is a chance to adjust the input in the next forecast cycle. But there is still no guarantee that this forecast will be properly implemented. Very often the forecast will be adjusted by production based on raw material availability or on capacity planning variables within the plant.

Then there is the sales order process. There is no point in customer service operators giving misleading information to customers. The process they follow must follow the guidelines on lead times, stock availability and so on set out by the inventory management personnel earlier in the process.

And we must be confident in our ability to execute the plan. Procurement will need to source the raw materials and components required of our plans. Production will need to be able to make product according to the plans and forecasts delivered. And finally there must be an ability to deliver to the customer after the product is made. This might seem obvious, but there are many cases where it is not simple. In the US a number of major courier companies were unable to deliver millions of orders in time for Christmas 2014. In many countries there are problems delivering to remote areas. In one extreme case a wind turbine manufacturer was unable to deliver its wind turbines because the dispatch department had not properly planned the delivery route. The result was that the giant blades required could not be manoeuvred under low bridges or through tight ravines. In one case diggers had to be used to build a temporary road that would deliver the product. This is becoming an increasing problem in our internet age of home delivery for almost everything. In the UK this became an extreme problem at the end of 2014. So many companies have jumped into the home delivery space that delivery rates plunged. This has resulted in very low incomes for the army of independent delivery companies, many of which are one man bands, and the closure of one major company, City Link, just before the festive season was complete.

7 The Remaining Inventories

If you have managed to optimise your inventories you will be still left with something. The size of the inventories you have will be determined by your manufacturing footprint. The more complex your process the more likely that you will still have a sizeable amount of stock. There are even some who have tried to develop a business model where products are manufactured and sold but there is no inventory. This was the dream of the dot.com'ers of the late 1990's but even they found that it was almost impossible to develop a large multinational business delivering products to customers where no inventory would exist. Although some tried hard they found it difficult to be guilty for the faults of their various drop-shippers and many lost heart and business as a result. Some have been more successful than others. Dell Computer based their model on an outsourced supply chain where they would never touch the product. To this day Dell are still very good at keeping their inventories very low but they have never achieved the holy grail of zero inventory.

The big banks dabbled with the idea of inventory financing in the past. There were largely two problems with the offering from the banks' perspective. The first was the risk of the stock becoming obsolete while it existed on their books. Banks will freely admit that they do not understand businesses in a deep manner and no universal formula could be found to calculate the risk of obsolescence. If you think like a banker and you cannot define risk properly, then you cannot price that risk. There were some attempts at this but all failed and for a number of years the big banks put this kind of offering in the "too difficult" box.

In the last two years this attitude from the major global banks has started to change. They still recognise that stock obsolescence can be a problem but now "Big Data" has arrived. In the world of Big Data the risk should be minimised for the bank as long as the bank knows where the stock is at all times. In theory anyone with a decent ERP system should be able to fulfil this requirement. But for those who run supply chains using such ERP systems there are a number of problems that mean you may not know where your inventory is or how much you have at a given time. At one company, we wanted to understand the holding of spare parts. We were told that they estimated that there were 150,000 spare parts but they could not be sure. This was for a number of reasons. Some parts were so old they were not sure if they were ever recorded properly. In many cases the same part would be recorded numerous times under different part numbers. In some other cases the parts were recorded in the ERP but could not be physically found on the shop floor. These are not unusual problems. For manufacturing stocks it is vital to have control over inventory accuracy. Regular stock counts always surface errors and always will as long as people are involved. This will happen because people will pick the wrong stock item, the unit of measure recorded will be wrong, the item was placed in the wrong location, the item movement was not recorded properly in the ERP system or returns are not properly processed. And there are many more errors that can happen. These are problems that Big Data cannot solve.

But let us assume that none of the above are a problem, then the assumption of Big Data is that you simply extract the data into your reporting tool and you suddenly know where everything is at all times. Unfortunately, as alluded to in the section on Working Capital Reporting, the vast majority of companies are not very good at reporting transactional information in their businesses and this is particularly acute for the reporting of inventory. For all the money spend on reporting systems, there are still too many companies that are unable to report effectively on the status of their inventories. But without this seemingly basic requirement then a bank will deem you to be too much of a risk to do any inventory financing deal.

But again let us assume that you have overcome this hurdle there is still the tricky subject of risk ratings. By the end of 2009 only four companies in the S&P 500 had a risk rating of AAA. They were ADP, Johnson & Johnson, Microsoft and ExxonMobil. Out of thousands of companies this is a very small group. Since 2009 many banks have ended major banking relationships with companies that they deem to be too high risk. In parallel all the major banks are being stress tested and the results of those tests are being regularly published. So it has become in a banks best interest to be highly risk averse and to move their loan book from companies deemed to be a higher risk to those with a much lower risk. This has largely meant that companies with an excellent debt profile are being bombarded with offers from banks to loan money to the exclusion of those with more average ratings. For this reason it is unlikely that inventory financing is going to be a breakthrough product in the short term, but circumstances can change.

All this intransigence from banks is forcing businesses to seek alternative sources of funding from start-ups. One interesting business is called Kickfurther. In their model they crowd-fund from retail investors and then allow investors to "buy" the inventories of selected businesses at a rate that is acceptable to each business. This is in a very early state right now but it shows that there are people out there willing to fill the niche.

8 Supplier Payment Terms

The days when companies can simply continue to extend supplier payment terms to levels of total incredulity are largely over. These companies started with terms of 30 and 45 days and then pushed to 60 days, then 90 days and some have stretched even further to 120 days. These changes have happened as their masters' demand more cash to be generated from the supply chain at the same time as pushing on price, quality and delivery performance. It was inevitable that at some point something had to give. Throughout 2014 the newspapers have learned that customers do not like buying from "supply chain bullies", as many of these companies have been perceived. The major retailers have been in the forefront of this debate, especially in Europe, where some had learned to be extraordinarily aggressive toward their own supply base. Some supermarkets have done considerable damage to their own brands and to the businesses that have supported their prosperity over the last 25 years.

In parallel to all this politicians have started to get in on the act. While there have been laws in place in a few countries to protect small companies, like in India and Japan, for many decades, the first serious law to enforce payment terms in business transaction happened in France in 2008. A law called Loi de Modernisation de l'Economie or LME was passed that imposed heavy fines for late payment, a maximum 60 day payment term for most business transactions and other lower payment terms for items such as transportation and perishable goods. Huge political pressure was put on major French companies to comply and the law was seen as being hugely successful. Although it should be stated that many smaller

French businesses have never implemented the law and there have been no prosecutions to date relating to this legislation.

Then the Spanish put their toes in the water. The Spanish law (15/2010) sought to gradually reduce the maximum payment term allowable from 85 days in 2010 to 60 days in 2013 with further exceptions for engineering contracts and a further 30 days maximum term for public bodies. This law has never been enforced in any way. I remember being at an internal company finance director conference where the discussion came up about the DSO targets of the various affiliate companies. The Spanish subsidary had agreed with Group management to a target DSO of 134 days. I then asked the question about the new law and why their DSO target was not 85 days or less. Group did not know about the new law and the local affiliate had no plan to tell them about it.

Then the European Parliament decided to get involved. They passed a Directive called 2011/7/EU or to give its more user friendly title: The European Directive on Combating Late Payment in Commercial Transactions. In general the Directive states that for most commercial transactions the maximum payment term is 60 days and for public sector transactions the maximum term is 30 days. And the Directive is not retrospective. So if the contract never changes then the Directive will never apply. This Directive has made things more difficult in that its consequences have been very different in different European countries. For example, in Denmark and Sweden any term above 30 days must be agreed by both parties in writing before it can be enacted, but no limit is placed on the number of days that can be agreed. Thus Dansk Supermarked issued a letter to their suppliers asking for 90 day payment terms that also threatened to end the supply relationship if this payment term was not agreed by the supplier. Although this didn't do the company's popularity any favours, it was completely within the law. In the UK, the Westminster Parliament transposed the Directive without any meaningful debate. This has proved to be important since the law now states that any term above 60 days will be deemed unfair if the term constitutes "any gross deviation from good commercial practice, contrary to good faith and fair dealing". This might seem fairly innocuous, but in British law there is no implicit assumption of good faith and fair dealing in a contract. This means that technically someone could agree a term above 60 days. In Italy, Spain and Portugal the law has been completely ignored and there is no-one from either the public sector, who have little cash to comply with the law, or from the large private sector companies, who routinely pay their smaller suppliers between 75 and 120 days. There are still many businesses across Europe who are still unaware of the Directive. So in summary, this was a nice idea that has not been well drafted and lacks political will in many countries to see that it is enforced.

The United States is trying a different approach. President Obama has started an initiative called SupplierPay. Under this scheme a number of companies like Apple, Johnson & Johnson and FedEx have pledged to pay smaller suppliers on short terms. This all sounds very generous until you understand that early payment comes at a price. The small business will only be paid after paying a finance fee. The theory is that it allows small companies without brilliant credit ratings to get paid early at a relatively cheap rate without hurting the DPO of the big company. So for many small companies that are operating on small margins this will seem like another additional cost they have to pay. So it remains true that there are no free lunches.

9 Payment Timing

One of the biggest reasons for paying invoices before due date is that an internal manager has made some kind of request to Accounts Payable. The Accounts Payable people tend to follow orders, so they execute the instruction. Many companies do not even report on early payment so they have no idea whether it goes on or how much damage is being done to the working capital profile. This problem is easily solved. Firstly have a report in place that identifies every single invoice that has been paid before due date and its associated cost centre. Then each cost centre manager should need to report why the invoice was paid early and to a very high authority. In one US assignment this high authority was the CFO of a $30 billion company. This move scared the hell out of everyone and the practice went from being endemic to exceptional overnight.

The next thing to do is to abolish the daily payment run, except for those invoices where a discount is earned. Many companies now only pay weekly or every second week and a handful only pay monthly. Assuming that invoices are only ever paid on or after due date then weekly payments should increase your DPO by 3 to 4 days. Paying every second week will increase your DPO by about 7 days and paying monthly will increase your DPO by around 15 days. Not every company will be able to do this, but at least weekly should be doable for the vast majority of companies. If this path is taken then it is important to allow for exceptions. There will be occasions when a payment needs to be made quickly and there should be a route for that to happen. But the route should be made difficult so that only a few senior staff are able to initiate such payments.

A common problem amongst some very large corporations is what is called "pulling forward". Imagine that you run a weekly payment run every Friday. When you set up the payment run in your ERP then you must set up some payment parameters. One of those parameters will be the latest invoice due date allowable for that payment run. Best practice says that the latest allowable due date should be the date of the payment run, i.e. we would only select cleared invoices with due dates up to and Including Friday's date. But at some companies the latest allowable due date is up to the day before the next payment run, i.e. We would select all cleared invoices with a due date up to Thursday of the following week. Some might say that there is an element of the gamekeeper turning into the poacher with this point and that is certainly true. But if your objective is to have the lowest working capital number possible then best practice should be followed.

The final and most important step to be taken to improve working capital through the adjustment of payment timings is adjusting how due dates are calculated. Many years ago when working at an aerospace client we examined their terms and conditions of payment and it said that a cleared invoice would be paid on a due date calculated based on the invoice date plus the agreed payment term unless the invoice was received more than 7 days after the invoice date. But this term had not been implemented in their payment system. Instead their ERP system calculated due dates based on the invoice date plus the agreed term. In those days most invoices were still being received on paper and it was quite a job to capture the actual invoice receipt date. Once we had achieved this, we then needed the programmers to write an overnight batch programme that would review all invoices that had been cleared that day and recalculate their due dates based on the invoice receipt date and not the invoice date. Once implemented this project stream delivered nearly half of all the benefit from the payables stream of the working capital programme. There were many sceptics. Surely the benefit would only be 2 or 3 days? The evidence based on invoice analysis showed the gap between invoice date and invoice receipt date averaged between 11 and 13 days in any given month and in more than 75% of cases the gap was greater than 7 days. Would suppliers get smart to the process and simply change how they bill? Analysis showed that only 5% of suppliers changed their billing routines in response to the change. This includes those who switched to various forms of electronic billing to avoid the gap between the dates. Then we were told that it was unfair. Again analysis showed that of all invoices paid late before the change up to 50% of late payments were caused by the supplier delivering the invoice late. In fact in many cases the invoice was not delivered until after the original due date. So we saw the change as a means of imposing a process discipline on suppliers.

As mentioned earlier one of the hardest things to establish with paper invoices is the actual invoice receipt date. This is because ERP systems will record the input date, but not the receipt date. Thankfully now most large companies have implemented some form of electronic invoice capture for almost all invoices. This ranges from EDI invoices to various scanning solutions. This means that there is an electronic record now of almost all invoices received making it that much easier to implement this solution.

10 Supply Chain Finance

Supply Chain Finance is not a new idea. In very basic terms a supplier sends you an invoice. Once the invoiced is approved it becomes a confirmed invoice, i.e. the only reason this invoice is not being paid now is that it is not due for payment. The supplier then gets a choice: wait for payment at the original due date or get paid more quickly in return for a financing fee. The theory is that the supplier will pay a fee that is equivalent to their customer's cost of finance. In most cases if the customer company is a large corporation then it should be able to borrow at a lower rate than the smaller supplier company. If so, this can mean a relatively cheap form of lending for the small supplier company. In theory such schemes are "no brainers". If that is the case then why don't all major corporations have a supply chain finance scheme?

The reality is that very few companies have launched large scale successful schemes that have made a noticeable difference to the working capital result. The first problem is with invoice processing. If the invoice is not confirmed then it cannot be part of the scheme. Sometimes this will be because there are delays in authorising invoices, but it could also be that you are in an industry that inherently has large numbers of invoice disputes or deductions. Having many disputes raised against invoices that may already be confirmed can cause big processing headaches. The next problem can be that suppliers might like the idea of the scheme but want some kind of guarantee that the liquidity to fund the scheme will be available for the longer term. No-one will be prepared to give such assurances so a supplier may choose to continue with more expensive funding options as a result.

In my experience there are lots of companies who officially have a supply chain finance programme in place but who have not pushed it aggressively enough into their supply base. It is very common that a scheme exists and is only being utilised by a small number of suppliers. So companies that engage in such schemes need to ensure that their procurement community understand the scheme and are targeted to sign up as many suppliers as possible. For many procurement organisations supply chain finance can be seen as noise in the system since it does very little to improve prices, quality or any of the other measures that procurement is usually measured against. So why go to a lot of effort for something that potentially has no reward? So it is important to ensure that procurement is appropriately incentivised to support and maintain such a scheme over time.

In many older schemes the bank providing the liquidity was also responsible for underwriting the debt. So many smaller suppliers that failed the credit risk assessment of the bank were barred from the scheme. For procurement, this could be seen as a massive amount of time wasted and would prove to be a discouragement to sign up more suppliers. Most schemes now are underwritten by the customer company. So the customer company is free to choose who is part of the scheme even if they would have failed the banks risk assessment.

But there is still the barrier of you auditors. For such a scheme to work it must be possible to classify the accounts payable balance that is part of the supply chain finance scheme as accounts payable and not as debt. In most cases this should not be a problem but according to International Accounting Standards (IAS 39) there must not be a substantial difference between the original value of the payable amount and the ultimate amount paid by the company running the supply chain finance scheme. This is by no means a universal truth and different auditors may have different views on the specific scheme in different circumstances. So it is always wise to gain approval for the scheme from your auditors before you start. That will prevent some potentially nasty accounting surprises later in the process.

Many think that implementing a supply chain finance programme is a difficult piece of technology. Increasingly this is untrue. There are many providers now including major banks and software companies that can have their processes up and running with remarkable speed. The hardest part in setting up a successful scheme is getting high rates of supplier adoption. This is more of a change management programme than a technology programme. As mentioned earlier the key is to incentivise procurement to sign up large numbers of suppliers.

The final point that should be remembered in relation to supply chain finance schemes is that they should be a last step in a payables programme focused on releasing working capital and not the first. Done too early in proceedings such a scheme may block you from gaining full value from changing payment terms or payment timings.

11 Vision

An unfortunate fact of working capital management is that in the last 20 years only a handful of companies across the globe have made consistent improvements in working capital performance in every year that has been measured. Given that many more people know about the subject and that technology is ceaselessly moving the boundaries forward of what can be possible this should not be the case.

The vast majority of companies start a working capital programme because of a short term problem. Business rescue experts have long been using working capital management techniques to help turn around failing businesses. After the last big downturn in late 2008 there was a surge of working capital projects as many companies scrambled to reduce inventories and bloated receivables assets. But for many of these companies they took their short term medicine, working capital improved, in some cases substantially, and because the change was not fully embedded in the culture of the organisation the old bad habits soon started to re-occur. So a few years on from the initiative many of the gains have been lost. At one aerospace client where they had implemented 60 day terms with all of their suppliers in the early 1990's the percentage of payments on these terms had fallen to 43% after 12 years. And nobody knew. Other business issues had taken priority and working capital was considered to be something that had been triumphed years before.

I have come across many people in my career that learned about working capital management in one role and have subsequently taken the lessons forward into subsequent businesses they have joined. And very often these businesses are very unconnected and as diverse as FMCG products and commercial shipping to oil platform generators and motor racing teams.

Only a very few start a working capital programme with a true sense of vision. These are the companies that will succeed the most and are most likely to sustain the improvement. One example would be a top 10 global pharmaceutical company. This is a company that is very profitable and produces huge amounts of cash. They embarked of a working capital programme knowing it would take several years to get everything in place and to break down the internal resistance to change. Every time their CEO makes comments on their published results working capital and its importance is mentioned. There are screens in every company premises worldwide spreading the same message including videos of the CEO. No-one in this organisation can be in any doubt of the importance of working capital. This has allowed the people running the working capital programme to reduce working capital in the order of billions. So why would a cash rich and profitable organisation be interested in working capital? The answer is that they had the strategic vision to recognise that the demand for dividends was going up, the cost of acquisition for biotech companies was going up, the long term profit margins for pharmaceuticals was going down as margins decrease in developed countries and the competition with generic drugs in developing countries becomes stiffer. To be fair to the other major pharmaceutical companies, they have all recognised the same strategic drivers and as a result they all have some kind of working capital programme. But nowhere else have I seen the same drive and determination to succeed at working capital.

So whether you have low levels of working capital or no working capital is far less dependent on your industry sector or your business model. Even the most capital intensive industries have the opportunity to become working capital stars. The basic techniques are well established, technology means that we can better monitor progress and innovative financial tools from both banks and software companies are creating new options and methods to manage and reduce working capital levels.

But still many companies believe that they cannot make such progress or that working capital is not that important. The truth is that the gap between those companies that are the top performers and those companies who would be considered average performers widens every year. In a global village where all of us are exposed to currency fluctuations, supply chain risk and uncertain growth it is more and more important to manage working capital well. Those with cash will survive all economic storms, even the ones with otherwise bad ideas. So in a world where cash continues to be king it is your choice whether you want to be a working capital leader or a working capital laggard.

About the Author

Brian Shanahan is the leader and founder of Informita. Informita was formed in 2012 to assist companies in the areas of working capital and procurement, focusing on analytics, implementation and advisory. The team is there to support your working capital and procurement programmes from cradle to grave in a cost efficient and effective manner. Informita's clients include a number of world majors in food products, pharmaceuticals, construction, paper and media industries.

Before Informita, Brian spent 19 years in management consultancy, 5 years in financial accounting roles in the UK and 3 years in retail in Ireland. To date Brian has worked with nearly two hundred clients in 35 countries across 4 continents.

Brian is also the founder of TermsCheck.com, a service that allows you to compare customer and supplier payment terms with other companies' actual terms that have been compiled in 184 countries.

Brian is also the co-founder of The Working Capital Channel. This is a co-operation between Informita and a Belgian software company DiscoverEdge. DiscoverEdge's lead product is called CashForce. This is a big data tool for cash forecasting, working capital reporting and cash collection management.

In the media, Brian has been quoted many times in the financial press in such publications as The Financial Times, CFO Magazine Belgium, CFO World, The Manufacturer, The Grocer, Finance Director, Euromoney, Accountancy Age, Financial i and The Evening Standard. Brian has also appeared on CNBC Europe's Power Lunch to discuss working capital trends.

Contacts

If you would like more information on working capital please feel to contact us in the following ways:

Website:	www.informita.com
	www.termscheck.com
Email:	info@informita.com
Phone:	+44-20-3286-4109
Twitter/Facebook:	@informita

Other Publications by Brian Shanahan

The Working Capital Handbook

The Procurement Leader's Handbook

Working Capital: What's Next?

Achieving Change